A SHORT HISTORY OF THE

ROCK ISLAND PRISON BARRACKS

(Revised Edition)

BY

Otis Bryan England

Historical Office
US Army Armament, Munitions, and Chemical Command
Rock Island, Illinois 61299-6000
1985

PREFACE

Nothing is stagnant; not even history. As continued research clears the mists of time, more of our past comes into focus.

This pamphlet was originally written in 1981 to answer continual public inquiries for information on the prison camp for Confederate soldiers that existed on Arsenal Island from 1863 to 1865. While the life of the camp was relatively short, the Rock Island Barracks stirred a controversy that long outlived it. Popular fiction and news articles presented a picture of the prison as an "Andersonville of the North." But was it a Northern counterpart to the Southern "hell hole," or was it merely a reflection of all prisoner of war camps of the period? The original A Short History of the Rock Island Prison Barracks, while far from being a definitive work, suggested the latter.

Since that time the author has benefited from research on the prison in the holdings of the National Archives, and from the writings of others who have delved into the somewhat esoteric subject of Civil War prisons. Continuing public requests for the pamphlet and a diminishing stock provided the opportunity of revising and expanding it. This revised edition of A Short History of the Rock Island Prison Barracks is the end result.

For the most part, all quotations used in this pamphlet have left the original spelling and punctuation intact. Additionally, all reference citations appear at the back of the pamphlet, to prevent breaks in the continuity of the work.

The author would like to thank Mr. James R. Cooper, Jr., who allowed time to be spent in this pamphlet's preparation that could have been spent on more pressing projects; Dr. Sheila C. Kamerick, Mr. Lawrence L. Leveque, and Mr. Dennis L. Noble, who read and made comments on the text; and Mrs. Carol L. Secoy, who generously donated her time to put the finishing touches on the manuscript. This pamphlet was printed by the Printing and Reproduction Division of the Rock Island Arsenal's Administrative and Community Activities Office, and the front cover and the map on page 2 were prepared by its Audio Visual Division. The author is indebted to their support.

OTIS BRYAN ENGLAND
October, 1985

A SHORT HISTORY OF THE
ROCK ISLAND PRISON BARRACKS

By the summer of 1863, all expectations that the Civil War would be a short campaign had faded to the realization that both sides were faced with a long, protracted conflict. With that realization came the problem of the security of large numbers of prisoners of war, a problem that had not previously been faced by the United States. The Dix-Hill Cartel for the mutual exchange of prisoners had been signed in July 1862, but both the North and the South selectively ignored or complied with the cartel in response to the success or failure of their efforts in the field. The side holding the greatest number of prisoners found itself reluctant to relinquish its relative superiority in trained combat troops, while the other side clamored for strict adherence to the cartel. The use of black troops by the North created additional strains on the agreement. Black prisoners of war were often sold back into slavery or were used extensively in manual labor, and the Confederate secretary of war expressed the opinion that the South should never be "inconvenienced" by having white officers of black regiments as prisoners. The North stopped exchanging prisoners, and ever-increasing numbers of them began to collect on both sides of the Mason-Dixon line. 1/

In the North, Confederate prisoners had initially been confined in prison camps located in the Midwest, but these had emptied in 1862 with the signing of the cartel. With the cartel's collapse, these camps reopened, and forts along the eastern seaboard were called into service as the numbers held in confinement grew. Even these were insufficient to contain all the prisoners, however, and the Union sought additional camps. Rock Island, Illinois, isolated in the Mississippi River, far from the battle areas, and largely controlled by the government since its designation as a national arsenal in July 1862, proved an ideal location for such a camp. In July 1863, Captain Charles A. Reynolds was ordered to Rock Island by Quartermaster General Montgomery C. Meigs to survey and to begin construction of a prison barracks of sufficient size to accomodate 10,000 prisoners of war. 2/

In August, Captain Reynolds began construction of the camp on the north central shore of the island. (See the illustration on the following page.) Almost immediately the prison camp became a part of the ongoing rivalry between the towns on the Iowa and Illinois sides of the river, and between their respective newspapers. The Rock Island, Illinois, Argus, aligned with the Democratic party, asked:

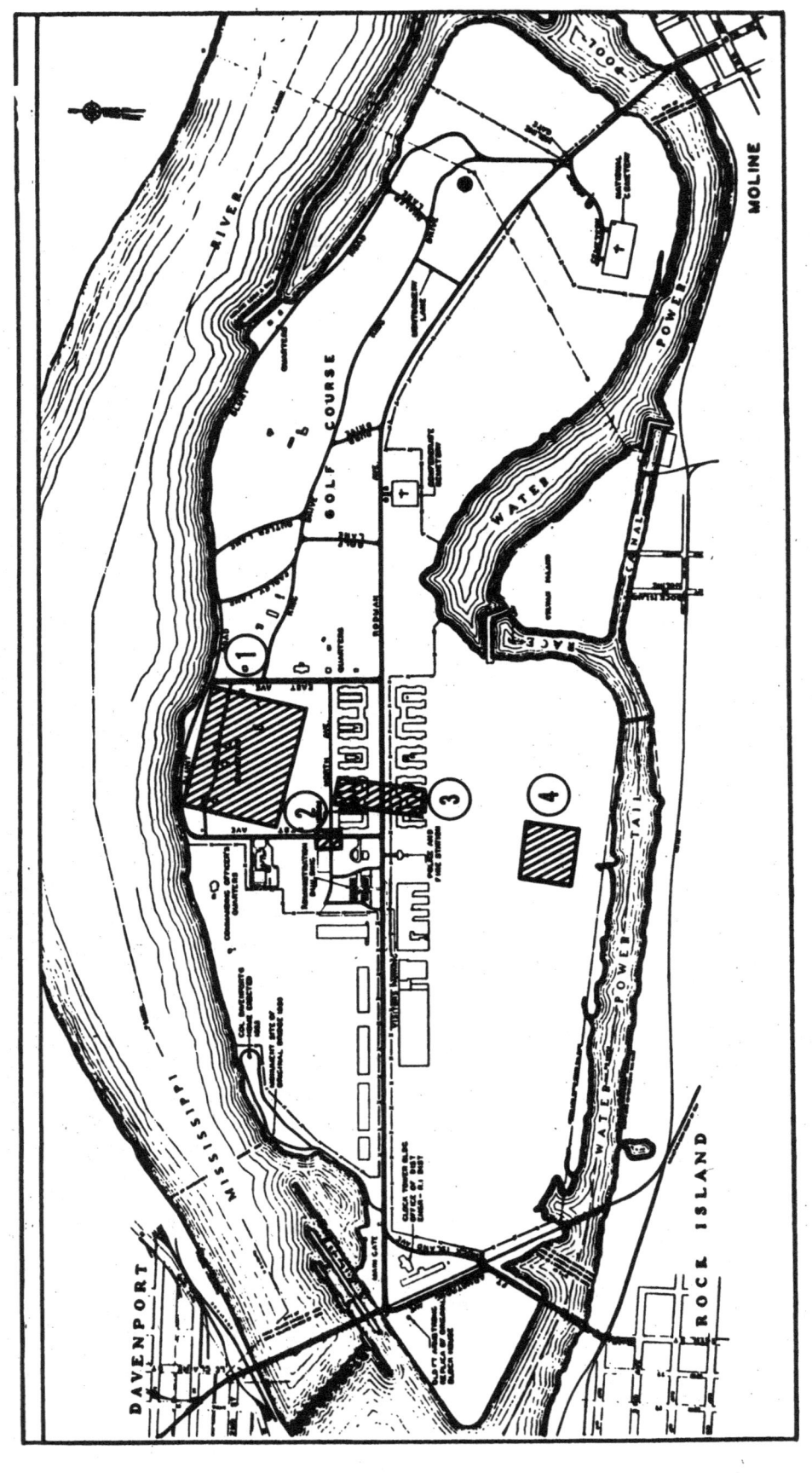

> Can anybody tell what influences were brought to bear to induce Capt. Reynolds to locate the military prisons on the north side of the Island, exposed to the bleak northwest winds, and in a position where they will be partially cut off from this end of the Island? . . . Was the proposed location, on the north side, selected to please Davenport [Iowa] political shoddy contractors? The situation of the Island, and its accessibility by a bridge, should be shown to the secretary of war before the work is commenced. The south side of the Island is the proper place for the barracks. 3/

The prison barracks proper consisted of eighty-four 22 by 100 feet buildings arranged in six north to south rows of fourteen buildings each. (See the illustration on the following page.) An 18 by 22 feet kitchen, with a stove for cooking, was located at the west end of each barracks, with the remaining 82 feet used for sleeping quarters for the 120 residents. A main east to west 90 feet-wide avenue bisected the camp and connected the two main gates. The entire stockade area was surrounded by a 12 feet high fence, with a sentry walk built 4 feet from the top on the outside of the fence, and sentry boxes placed every 100 feet. Additionally, ditches were dug on the north, east, and west sides of the camp to denote the "dead line," or the point at which a sentinel would shoot at an approaching prisoner, and to prevent the digging of tunnels. There was no ditch dug on the south side, since the nearness of bedrock to the surface was felt to be an adequate obstacle to tunneling. Instead, a row of stakes denoted the "dead line" on the south side of the stockade. 4/

The overcrowding at existing prison camps, exacerbated by a string of Union victories in the West, forced the Rock Island Barracks to be occupied before it was completely finished. The barracks for the guards, situated on the east and west sides of the prison compound, were still under construction when the first contingents, members of the Veteran Reserve Corps, began to arrive in mid-November 1863. When elements of the 37th Regiment Iowa Volunteers arrived in January 1864, the Davenport _Democrat_ reported that:

> . . . they found no preparation whatever made for them. There were no accomodations on the Island, and none in the city except vacant stores, halls etc., in which they were quartered. They brought with them rations enough to last until tomorrow. They will have to be colonized about the city of Rock Island until barracks are prepared for their reception.

ROCK ISLAND MILITARY PRISON.

Pesthouse.   Officers' Quarters.   Hospital.   Prison Barracks.   First Mississippi River Bridge.

As late as May 1864, seven buildings within the prison compound were being used to house six companies of the 37th and their laundresses. Even the post headquarters building was not completed until the latter part of May, when increasing pressure from the arsenal commander, Major Charles P. Kingsbury, forced the prison commander, Colonel Adolphus J. Johnson, to vacate a house on the west end of the island built by area pioneer George Davenport. 5/

Despite the condition of the prison, the first shipment of Confederate prisoners arrived on 3 December 1863. A witness to the arrival left this report.

> It was on a dark, raw, gloomy day, December 3, 1863, when the first Confederate prisoners came. I promise you, it was a day fraught with intense excitement, never to be forgotten. . . It was known that the "prisoners' train" was to be run on the island to a certain point, switched off, and [the prisoners] disembarked and marched to the prison, a mile away. Hundreds of Rock Island and Davenport citizens stood waiting at the designated place. A strong, thick cable of rope was run to keep the people back. The police of both cities were out in full force, with deputies sworn in. 6/

By the end of December, the original 468 prisoners, captured at the battle of Lookout Mountain in Tennessee, had swollen to almost 5,600. This surge of population created massive problems for the still disorganized prison administration, which was faced with trying to cope with one of the worst winters on record. The prison's stock of issue clothing and blankets was quickly depleted by the large number of prisoners who were ill-prepared to face a northern winter, and while the supply of coal was adequate to fuel the two heating stoves and one kitchen stove per barrack, it was necessary to impress teams to transfer it from the coal house to the barracks on a least one occasion - a move that caused the Rock Island *Argus* to report:

> NO CAUSE FOR ALARM--We hear that many people from the country do not come to town with their teams for fear they will be impressed into the government service as were a few during the terrible storm of last week. This impression is producing a bad effect on the business of the city and ought to be counteracted at once.
>
> Lieut. Col. Schaffner, who has charge of that department at the barracks, assures us that it was with very great reluctance that he resorted to that mode of

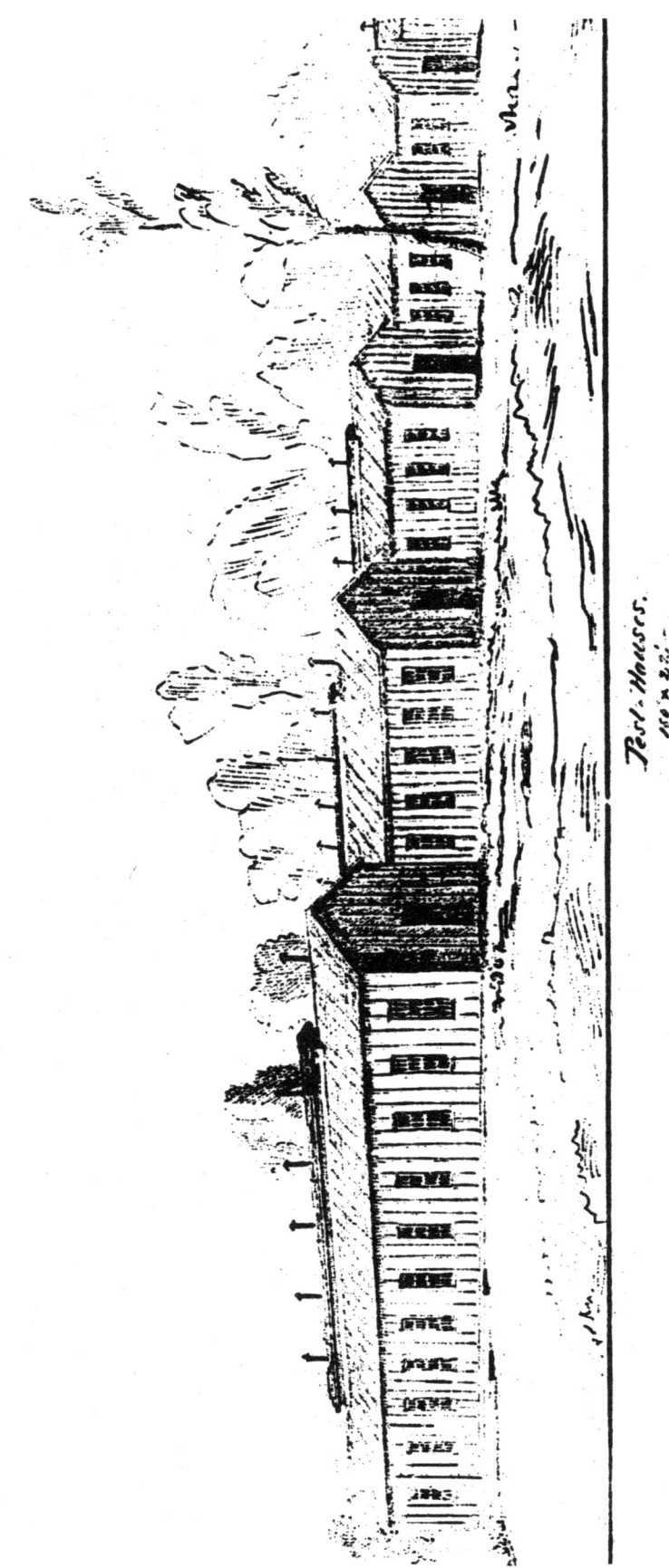

Contemporary drawing of variola hospital or "pest houses"

obtaining teams, but it was an absolute necessity to do so, at that time, or the prisoners of war would have suffered severely from the cold. But he says he has now made such arrangements as will positively prevent a similar occurence, and that there is no probability that such an event will ever occur again. No one, therefore, need fear to come to town on the account named, for their is no sort of danger of the kind named. . . 7/

The major problem the camp's administration faced, however, came in with the prisoners. In the first contingents to arrive, the prison doctors found 94 cases of smallpox, to which all the prisoners had been exposed. The prison staff had an insufficient supply of medicines and vaccine to fight the plague, and a hospital for the prisoners had not been built! As a consequence, the sick remained in the same barracks with the healthy, and the disease continued to spread. Smallpox, together with pneumonia and diarrhia, claimed 98 prisoners and 3 guards during the month of December, 231 prisoners and 4 guards in January 1864, and 350 prisoners and 10 guards in February. 8/

In early February 1864, the camp was inspected by Assistant Surgeon General A. M. Clark, who immediately began to take corrective measures. Clark first isolated the sick from the healthy by causing 11 barracks on the southwest side of the stockade to be fenced off from the rest of the compound to serve as a prison hospital. He also directed the construction of six "pest houses" on the south side of the island for those patients with virulent diseases. Clark then directed that the Confederate dead, which had been buried about 100 yards south of the prison compound, be exhumed and moved to the present site of the Confederate Cemetery, while the Union dead were buried about 500 feet to the northwest of that. Finally, Clark authorized the construction of a prison hospital of 560 beds, which could be crowded to 700 beds in an emergency. However, Commissary-General of Prisoners William Hoffman suspended the construction of the hospital "evidently from the impression that the amount of sickness was principally due to smallpox and of a temporary character. . . " 9/

Colonel William Hoffman of the 3rd Infantry Regiment, an officer on parole after having been captured at San Antonio, Texas, at the outbreak of the war, had been named commissary--general of prisoners in October 1861 to give some semblance of order to the Union prison system, selecting sites for the prisons and establishing regulations for their management. Hoffman, born in 1807, had graduated from West Point in 1829; eighteenth in a class of forty-six, behind Cadets Robert E. Lee and Joseph E. Johnston. He served with the 6th Infantry during the Black Hawk War, which may have familiarized him with Rock Island and influenced his later decision to establish a prison upon it. He

Colonel William Hoffman, Commissary-General of Prisoners

served with distinction in the war with Mexico, and was breveted twice for "gallant and meritorious conduct" at the battles of Contreras, Churubusco, and Molino del Rey. 10/

The medical problems of the Rock Island Barracks also came to the attention of the medical director of the Northern Department, Surgeon Charles S. Tripler, who called for a special report on "the causes of this mortality," and who in turn passed the report on to the acting surgeon-general. In his report, Surgeon William Watson, who had replaced the somewhat inexperienced Assistant Surgeon M. K. Moxley as surgeon in chief on 4 March, stated that he had found 350 prisoners sick in quarters and 715 in the makeshift prison hospital, 420 of which were in the "pest houses." The current prison population was about 7,600. Watson wrote:

> I found a great want of cleanliness among the patients and attendants, which is disappearing under stringent regulations requiring the regular use of bath tubs and the labors of a permanent detail as laundrymen. The good effects of this is most apparent in the smallpox wards, where the impression seemed to prevail that it was injurious to wash, which resulted in an accumulation of filth that, in connection with the disease, suspended entirely the functions of the skin, producing congestion in cases that might have progressed without unpleasant symptoms . . .

Watson stated that "everything has been done by the medical officers, and all their efforts had been promptly seconded by Col. A. J. Johnson, commanding the post, to check the spread of smallpox and mitigate the severity of other diseases." In an included report to Colonel Johnson, Watson pleaded for the completion of the prison hospital.

> . . . Feeling that every principle of honor and humanity dictates that no effort should be spared to save the lives of those suffering, misguided men whom the chances of war have thrown into their present position, has induced me to make this communication. 11/

The cost-conscious Colonel Hoffman yielded to the pressure exerted by the surgeon-general's office, and notified Johnson in early April that the building of the prison hospital had been approved, the expense to be paid from the prison fund. "You will continue, therefore, the work," he wrote, "and let it be completed with as little delay as practicable, observing the closest economy in all things." 12/

Surgeon Clark again inspected the prison in early April 1864, and while he found conditions somewhat improved, there were still some needed changes. While Clark found the barracks to be warm and properly ventilated, the "police of the barracks is not as strictly attended to as it was at the time of my last inspection, nor are the men as cleanly." Additionally, Clark found that:

> . . . the police of the grounds is bad except on the central avenue. In the neighborhood of many of the barracks the refuse of the kitchens is scattered on the ground about the doors instead of being collected in proper receptacles.

The general lack of cleanliness included the prison hospital, still inside the prison stockade and plagued with a drainage problem, since it occupied the lowest section of the camp.

> Every principle of humanity and a due regard to the preservation of human life demands that the sick should be removed from these quarters at the earliest possible moment--at any rate before the hot weather sets in--and in this opinion I am sure the Commissary-General of Prisoners would coincide on a personal inspection. 13/

Clark found the smallpox or variola hospital in good condition, but the lack of clothing in the camp posed a problem.

> . . . From the lack of an adequate supply of clothing with which to provide convalescents on returning to quarters, the surgeon in charge has attempted to purify and disinfect the clothing brought by them to the pest--house. This is done by thoroughly boiling the clothes, then subjecting them in a close apartment to the fumes of burning sulphur, followed by a second boiling. This is said to have been effectual in destroying the infection, as no new case has yet been traced to the use of this clothing. The process may be effectual, still I do not think it safe to trust to it. New clothing should be furnished to all returning to quarters.

While the plague had abated somewhat, Clark was still far from satisfied. The vaccination program for prisoners he found to be "not as effectual as it should be owing to the inferior quality of the vaccine virus provided by the medical purveyor." 14/

The lack of cleanliness was not limited to the prison stockade, however. Upon inspecting the living accomodations for the guards, Clark reported:

> . . . The police of the barracks is generally bad, especially in those occupied by the Thirty-seventh Iowa Volunteers. The kitchens and utensils are not in very good order, and in many places the kitchen refuse is scattered on the ground instead of being collected in proper receptacles. Many of the bunks are closely boarded up, to the detriment of the health of the men occupying them. Many of the barracks are very insufficiently ventilated.
>
> The ground about the garrison barracks is in many places in very poor police. 15/

Colonel Hoffman reacted to Clark's report by directing Johnson to:

> . . . Hereafter have a weekly report made by the officer in charge of the prisoners of the condition of the police of the barracks, hospitals, outhouses and grounds and forward it to this office with your remarks. Keep me advised at these times of all that you are doing to keep the depot in a creditable condition. 16/

The office of the commissary-general of prisoners was not the only critical eye turned toward the Rock Island Barracks, however. In mid-April 1864, Lieutenant Colonel John F. Marsh conducted an inspection for the office of the inspector general. Colonel Marsh found the prison stockade:

> . . . in excellent condition; discipline and government good; barracks clean; grounds thoroughly policed, and being constantly improved by grading and drainage. The shelter, food, clothing, and treatment for the health of the prisoners is good. . .

The inspector was not so generous in his comments about the prison garrison, however.

> Commanding officer, Col. A. J. Johnson, Fourth Regiment Veteran Reserve Corps. Colonel Johnson is intelligent and a man of good habits, but not as efficient as he ought to be. The troops under his command are not properly instructed in guard duty or in the method of keeping their books, making returns, &c. The grounds surrounding the barracks are neglected. . .
>
> Troops composing garrison, Fourth Regiment Veteran Reserve Corps and Thirty-seventh Iowa Volunteers; the latter a regiment of decrepit old men and the most unpromising subjects for soldiers I ever saw. . .

> Post quartermaster, Capt. Charles A. Reynolds, U.S. Army. Returns for March not finished. Could not ascertain what balance was due United States. The captain was somewhat intoxicated. 17/

In his endorsement to Colonel Marsh's report, the inspector general informed Colonel Hoffman that Colonel Johnson:

> . . . has been directed to properly instruct his command and to cause the grounds in the vicinity of his post to be cleaned. General Meigs, Quartermaster-General, has been ordered to relieve Capt. Charles A. Reynolds from his duty as post quartermaster, and to designate an officer to receive his money and property.

It was the middle of June, however, before Reynolds was relieved and ordered to Nashville, Tennessee. 18/

Despite inefficiency in the post garrison, shortages of needed supplies, and hindrance from the commissary-general's office, the situation at the prison barracks was beginning to improve. By the middle of June, a prisoner stricken by an acute skin disease could note in his diary: "Found hospital pleasant place & began to improve." Yet needed improvements were still hampered by obstructions from the cost-conscious Colonel Hoffman. In a letter to Colonel Johnson dated 5 June 1864, Hoffman wrote:

> . . . The instructions to Surgeon Clark did not contemplate that he would order the erection of so extensive a hospital without the approval of this office, and much less was it anticipated that he would authorize the erection of any building to be paid out of funds which had not yet been collected. Such an order could not be carried out except by such an arrangement as was made by Captain Reynolds, which was injudicious and not authorized, and should not have been entered into until it had been referred to the Quartermaster-General and this office for approval. I have understood that Captain Reynolds had been ordered to be relieved, which must necessarily lead to much embarrassment in the settlement of his accounts for these disbursements. In all my letters on this subject I have urged the observance of the strictest economy, but from the items given in the report to Captain Reynolds I am led to believe that the expense was not as much considered as it should have been. One building of fourteen rooms, plastered, seems to be an extravagent allowance for surgeons. A patent range at a cost of $600 is also an extravagent item. Of the other items I cannot well judge, but they seem to be on a too liberal scale; much

more so than is proper in providing for rebel prisoners. . . In your letter of the 9th ultimo you for the first time speak of a fence and a sentry walk and covered way. What are these to cost? 19/

Despite the hindrance, the 560 bed prison hospital was finished by the end of July. The prison hospital, consisting of 14 frame wards arranged in echelon, with an additional executive building, kitchen, laundry, and mess room, was located south of the prison compound and similarly encircled with a 12 feet high stockade fence. In addition, a post hospital was constructed for those of the garrison who became ill. The staff of the prison hospital consisted of Surgeon Watson, Assistant Surgeon Moxley, seven acting assistant surgeons, and two hospital stewards. Additionally, prisoners of war were used to make up the seven cooks and 87 nurses needed to operate the facility. 20/

In late July Surgeon C. T. Alexander inspected the camp and its hospitals and found conditions vastly improved. "The camp is well managed," he wrote. However, obstructionism from the commissary-general was still in evidence. Alexander reported:

> . . . It was the intention of the Government to have suitable water-works erected for supplying the entire camp with water. For some reason (misunderstanding as to the cost of the masonry of the reservoir, I am informed) this order had been countermanded. Should the work, upon which already much has been done, be completed, it would be a great advantage. The management of the sinks, as now, will do very well for the summer, but in winter, when everything is frozen, they must, unless placed over proper drainage, prove a great nuisance. Anything you may be pleased to do toward forwarding the completion of the water-works before winter will be of great advantages as to maintaining the now well-policed condition of the camp. . .

Alexander found the hospital, also to be well managed, and its staff to be efficient, with one exception--Acting Assistant Surgeon Henry F. Salter, whom Alexander felt "should be relieved as a sympathizer, suspected of carrying news and articles to prisoners . . ." 21/

So, by the end of July, 1864, the initial problems which had plagued the Rock Island Barracks had to a large extent been resolved. Construction on the barracks for the garrison was finished, an efficient hospital had been established, and the prison population, now at its peak of about 8,600 prisoners, at least reasonably safe from the scourge of disease that had decimated it. But to a great extent, the damage had already been

ROCK ISLAND MILITARY PRISON SCENES.

1. Bell Tower, Outside Entrance.
2. Prisoners Suffering Punishment Inflicted by Their Own Courts.
3. Administering the Oath of Allegiance.
4. View within the Stockade.
5. Prisoners Making Clam-Shell Trinkets.

done. The Confederate Cemetery now had a population of over 1,300, fully two-thirds of the prisoner deaths that were to occur during the life of the camp, which had been in existence only eight months. If any blame for these deaths must be placed, it must rest on the shoulders of those who ordered prisoners into a camp that was not prepared to accept them, and who dragged their feet in taking corrective measures. 22/

The average prisoner at the Rock Island Barracks was faced with combating the boredom inherent in the life of all prisoners. While the island was far from a summer camp, there were ways to lighten the burden of passing time. There was a prison library, stocked by sympathetic citizens from the surrounding communities. Church services, presided over by visiting ministers from the surrounding area and by the post chaplain, distinguished the Sabbath from the other days of the week. Many prisoners engaged in the industry of making buttons and ornaments from shells and other materials to sell for whatever the market would bear. Prisoners were allowed to hold judicial proceedings to try crimes such as theft, and barracks lawyers often made the trials quite diverting. Additionally, there was the ever present hobby of speculating on the progress of the war, fed by newspapers smuggled into camp and rumors from the prison "grapevine." In one prisoner's words:

> . . . I would not have you think that [imprisonment] entirely crushed the spirits of our fellows, for many were the hours of revelry spent within these prison walls, enjoying the music of the improvised fiddles and listening to the stories told. Social lines were drawn, as in any body of people, and congenial spirits were sought in every walk of life . . . 23/

For those willing to work, there was the opportunity to make a small income by working on improvements on the camp itself. Captain Reynolds had run into financial difficulties in building the reservoir and sewer system for the camp and was reluctant to pay the prevailing wage of $1.50 to $1.75 per day for civilian labor to complete the system, and suggested using prisoner labor instead. Colonel Johnson passed on the suggestion to the commissary-general of prisoners with the recommendation that the laborers be paid $.40 per day for their services, the money to come out of the camp's prison fund. Colonel Hoffman referred the suggestion to the secretary of war, but recommended that the amount paid only be $.10 per day. To this the secretary agreed, with the provisio that prisoners so laboring be allowed full rations for combat troops. While somewhat limited in scope, the project at Rock Island marked one of only two Union experiments in the use of prisoner of war labor. 24/

Some prisoners at Rock Island, however, preferred to spend their time thinking of ways to end their captivity. Discounting a quick end to the war and their chances for exchange or parole, these prisoners decided to create their own exits from confinement. Forty-one successfully escaped during the life of the prison barracks, while many more made unsuccessful attempts, and a few died while trying to escape. 25/

Any analysis of the tales of escapes from the Rock Island Barracks is faced with several difficulties. Most accounts that have been found were published in the Confederate Veteran magazine about the turn of the 20th century, fully four decades after the accounts related. Both the cobwebs of time and the creative imaginations of the writers tended to obscure the facts of the escapes, and give them a swashbuckling air that failed to exist at the time.

A prime example may be found in the account of the escapes of Doctor Thomas F. Berry of Pauls Valley, Oklahoma. Dr. Berry claimed to have escaped "from eight different prisons and five times while on the way to Yankee prisons, escaping twice from Rock Island Prison, once on November 2, 1863," a feat not too difficult, since the first guards didn't arrive until the middle of the month. While Dr. Berry's mistake could be excused due to the passage of time, he destroyed this apology by stating, "My date is taken from a diary kept by me of those dark days of trials." In any event, Berry claimed to have escaped by crawling out of the camp's sewer system, but was recaptured in Cincinnati, Ohio, and returned to the camp. Berry claimed to have escaped again on 14 December 1864 by bribing a guard to turn his back while Berry and several other prisoners scaled the stockade fence. However, the guard betrayed them, and as they landed on the opposite side of the fence they saw "forty or fifty muskets, still, silent, ominous, and ready now to open with a deadly roar." According to Berry, four were killed, and one was "grievously wounded," but Berry and one companion managed to run to the half-frozen river and escape across it much like Eliza escaped in Uncle Tom's Cabin. Dr. Berry closed his account by contending, "I was wounded sixteen times in the Confederate service and five times in my foreign service--twenty-one wounds in all." 26/

In reality, Berry was captured on 14 June 1864 near Cynthiana, Kentucky, and escaped from the Rock Island Barracks on 4 December 1864; by crawling out through the camp's sewer system. He was never recaptured. 27/

Similar difficulties can be encountered in the attempted escape of B. M. Hord of Nashville, Tennessee. Hord attempted his escape by manufacturing a Union uniform from a stolen cap and blouse, and a pair of pants tailored from the stolen coat of the post sutler, who would sell goods to the prisoners. Hord finished his disguise by fabricating a pistol from a thick piece of pine board, then boldly walked out of the prison's main gate leading a detail of prisoners. Recaptured shortly thereafter, Hord claimed to have been locked in a "dungeon," consisting of an excavated hole in one of the guard houses, with a fellow prisoner who had killed another prisoner by striking him over the head with a board, and a black Union guard who had gone insane and opened fire on a squad of his own men, mortally wounding one of them. 28/

Much of Hord's story can be verified. The guard report for 7-8 November 1864 indicates that four people were confined to the post's guardhouse during that night; two Confederate prisoners under arrest for "murder," a black guard reported as "deranged," and another Confederate listed as "Ben Hoard." However, the only other prisoner who claimed to have been locked in the "dungeon" beneath the guard house was the indomitable Dr. Berry, who wrote his account after having read Hord's. 29/

Despite the fanciful aspects of some reported escapes, prisoners were able to effect their release prior to the date anticipated by the federal authorities. On 25 June 1864, Colonel Johnson was forced to report the following to Colonel Hoffman:

> COLONEL: I have the honor to report that on the night of the 14th instant ten prisoners of war made their escape from the prison inclosure by tunneling under Barracks 42, their egress being made directly under the parapet. The last two were discovered by the sentinel, who gave the alarm, and all necessary measures taken for their recapture, which has resulted in securing seven of them. Three were taken on the island, four near Rock River, about four miles distant, and one was drowned in attempting to cross the slough. Mounted patrols have been on the track of the remaining two until to-day, with fair prospect of taking them . . . The tunnel was made on the south side of the prison. Deep trenches had been made on the north, east, and west sides to prevent tunneling, it being deemed unnecessary to trench on the south side in consequence of the rock coming so near the surface. A trench has now been made down to the rock on that side also. 30/

While some escapes were elaborate and well planned, many were spur of the moment enterprises effected by burrowing under the compound fence or slipping off while on a work detail. In some instances these latter escapes were aided by the guard force. J. B. Hendricks and J. E. Tucker managed to escape while detailed with another prisoner to work on the roof of a small building outside the prison compound. While returning to the compound, the other prisoner told their guard that some of their tools had been left behind. According to Colonel Johnson, the prisoner then proposed:

> . . . that the guard should go back with him to get them, and the other two [Hendricks and Tucker] would wait till they returned. The Guard did so and in the mean time the two that were left behind vamoosed. The Guard is now in confinement and will be brought before the General Court Martial in session at this post for such gross neglect of duty and carelessness. 31/

Most prisoners planned their escapes for the balmy summer months, but a few hardy souls escaped into the rigors of the northern winter. David Sears, a local resident who owned a mill on the east side of the island remembered one such attempt a half century later.

> Early in 1864 four prisoners tunneled out on the north or river side of the prison. The night was dark and they walked up stream along the bank of the Mississippi river, and every now and then one of them would wade out into the river towards the Iowa shore until the water came up to his neck. Being unable to swim they had to turn back. When they reached our millrace near the dam from the island to Benham's island where the old Sear's mill stood, they found the water not to exceed four feet deep and succeeded in reaching Benham's island, thinking they had really crossed the river and were in Iowa. One of our teamsters, Ditmer Veitz on going out to the stable to get his team about midnight . . . saw two men dodge around the corner. He immediately ran to the mill which was running and notified the crew. They came armed with whatever they could find. It is said that the flour packer brought up the rear armed with a broom. They expected to find bold thieves but were astonished to see four cold and wet prisoners who immediately offered to surrender, and were taken into the mill. They were perishing from the cold and were glad of the opportunity to warm themselves at the big stove. Ice had begun to form on their clothing . . . 32/

Once he had successfully escaped from the island, however, a prisoner's chances of eluding recapture were increased by possible assistance from the area's population of rebel sympathizers, the most notable of which were Mrs. Charles Buford of Rock Island and Miss Kate Perry of Covington, Kentucky, who visited her cousin, a Mrs. Boyle of Rock Island, extensively during 1863-1864.

Initially the activities of rebel sympathizers in the local area were limited to providing a more comfortable existence to the prisoners, and to offering moral support. They eagerly responded to the post commander's pleas for donations of clothing and other necessities to help the prisoners weather the winter, and to augment their diet, a response that drew criticism from the pro-Republican Rock Island <u>Union</u>.

> . . . Yesterday there was considerable stir among the secesh inhabitants of Davenport and Rock Island, who sympathize with the rebel prisoners on the Island. These people, under the leadership of Judge Grant, a notorious copperhead, proceeded in a body to the Island, to distribute presents to the men who have been in the employ of Jeff. Davis, but who now are being dieted by Uncle Sam.--They showed their sympathy for the poor fellows who were so unfortunate as to have been taken prisoners by our loyal troops, by feeding them with choice nice tit [sic] bits, and caressing them with the smiles of approbation at what they had done--in the name of their masters, the Devil and Jeff Davis--by bestowing upon them liberally out of their abundances. 33/

According to her own account, Kate Perry used the call for aid to establish a veritable "underground" for procuring necessities for the prisoners.

> I began my work by writing to <u>all</u> my friends in Kentucky and everywhere else, asking for speedy aid. I wanted clothing and tobacco, the soldier's solace, but clothing especially. Then I begged all these friends to ask their friends, in the way establishing a sort of endless chain. Soon box after box of clothing and boxes of edibles began coming in . . . The contribution of clothing, shoes, tobacco, etc., continued to come in for months. 34/

The effectiveness of the sympathizers' campaign can be seen in the following notation, dated 13 February 1864, in Lafayette Rogan's diary:

> Liberal donations of clothing continue to be made by the good ladies of Ky, Ten, and by kind friends who do not reside far from this place. Mrs. Buford of R. I. is active in procuring necessaries. Miss Kate Perry of Ky has been here for weeks as a ministering angel. God bless all such and send more. 35/

Contemporary drawing of post headquarters

Miss Perry also smuggled notes into the camp using a Union Army sergeant, a post surgeon (see Alexander quotation on page 13), the driver of a milk wagon, and finally a Roman Catholic priest as couriers. 36/

It was a natural progression, therefore, to begin to aid escaping prisoners. One such prisoner was George Kern of Bourbon County, Kentucky, who managed to escape the prison barracks by holding onto the coupling pole of the chief surgeon's buggy, and riding out of the camp underneath the buggy much like Odysseus escaped from the cave of Polyphemus by clinging to the belly of a ram. When he appeared at Miss Perry's doorstep, she secreted him in the house for several days, and finally effected his escape from the region by using his small size and boyish looks (the prisoner was reportedly only fifteen) to disguise him as a girl, complete with hoop skirt and a scoop bonnet. Though her assistance to escaping prisoners was known to the local military authorities, Miss Perry was never arrested, though her house was the subject of persistent searches. 37/

Some conspirators were less fortunate. One group, a secret order calling itself the Order of American Knights and later the Order of the Sons of Liberty, plotted to seize the federal and state arsenals at Indianapolis, Columbus, and Springfield; to release prisoners of war at Rock Island and other western prison camps; and then to march into Kentucky and Missouri and join forces with the Confederate army. The plot was uncovered before any action could be taken, however, and the principal conspirators spent the remainder of the war in prison. 38/

One guard at the Rock Island Barracks claimed to have played a small role in uncovering the Sons of Liberty plot. W. T. Norton, later the first vice president of the Illinois State Historical Society, was detailed for a time at the provost marshal's office at the barracks, and censored mail going in and out of the prison. In September 1864, Norton claims, letters incorporating the use of invisible ink made from onions or the white of eggs were detected coming into and going out of the camp. Norton states:

> . . . Later on, when the gigantic plot for an uprising of the southern sympathizers in the north, the release of the confederates in northern prisons, and the burning of northern cities, was exposed, we knew what those letters meant . . . The copperheads of Rock Island and Davenport were in it up to their necks . . . 39/

Norton could be off on his dates, since his account was written a half century later and since the plot had actually been discovered by the September date he gives. Concern over prisoner uprisings was so great, however, that at one point Commissary-General of Prisoners Hoffman directed the building of a barge equipped with a 6-pounder field piece and a 24-pounder howitzer, to be anchored off the island as additional security. Hoffman wrote that "the object is to establish a floating citadel, inaccessible to the prisoners, and so armed as to overawe them." But in keeping with Hoffman's character, he added that it should be done "at as little expense as possible." When the barge arrived in Keokuk, Iowa, in October 1864, though, the water in the river was so low that the "floating citadel" could not be floated over the rapids. In January 1865, Colonel Johnson turned the barge over to the military authorities in Keokuk to prevent its "loss for want of proper care." 40/

In addition to the possibility of escape, there was another way for a prisoner of war to terminate his incarceration - to enlist in the armed services of the Union. Throughout the war, the Lincoln administration wavered between outright prohibition and full fledged support of efforts to enlist Confederate prisoners. The administration justly feared that ex-prisoners captured on the battlefield would be tried by Confederate authorities and shot as deserters. Pressure for prisoner recruitment continued to build, however, from politicians who feared the political repercussions of continued draft calls to maintain Union military strength. Finally the administration capitulated and launched an aggressive campaign to recruit Confederate prisoners of war for naval service, and for army service along the western frontier, far from the dangers of vengeful Confederate authorities. In all, between 6,000 and 10,000 of the estimated 150,000 Confederate prisoners chose this way of terminating their captivity. About 3,000 of those came from the Rock Island Barracks. 41/

Recruitment of prisoners at Rock Island began on 16 January 1864, when John D. Harty, a naval officer, arrived at the prison. Prisoners successfully recruited were immediately given the oath of allegiance, and were then transported to Boston or other east coast port cities to be assigned to vessels. 42/

Reaction to naval recruitment was astonishing. Within a week, over 660 prisoners had been recruited and shipped out. Lafayette Rogan's diary entry for February 9 ends with the following: "Navy Roll of 664 traitors to our country completed to day." By the end of the summer, over 1,000 rebel prisoners had entered the navy ranks. 43/

Possibly due to the success of navy recruitment and the fact that it was an election year, President Lincoln wrote to Secretary of War Stanton on 1 September 1864, that:

> It is represented to me that there are at Rock Island, Ill., as rebel prisoners of war, many persons of northern or foreign birth, who are unwilling to be exchanged and be sent South, but who wish to take the oath of allegiance and enter the military service of the Union.
>
> Colonel Huidekoper, on behalf of the people of some parts of Pennsylvania, wishes to pay the bounties the Government would have to pay to proper persons of this class, have them enter the service of the United States, and be credited to the localities furnishing the bounty money . . .

Lincoln then ordered that action be taken to comply with the request. 44/

Accordingly, a recruiting depot was opened at the prison on 11 September 1864, to procure soldiers to guard the Union's western frontier. Sixteen barracks were separated from the remainder of the stockade, and as prisoners were recruited, they were moved into the new compound. 45/

Many prisoners were eager to accept Uncle Sam's call. By the next day, Lafayette Rogan could write in his diary, "The heart grows sick and the soul sinks within me when I see so many deserting our cause," and he predicted that "From 1500 to 2000 of the prisoners here will enlist for frontier service." Rogan's prediction was extremely accurate, for within two months 1,797 prisoners had passed over the fence that separated the "Bull Pen" from the "Calf Pen," the area reserved for the new recruits, and several hundred more had been released from the prison after having been turned down for medical reasons. 46/

For many of the prisoners, the call for recruits was seen as the final step in a diabolical plot. Rations for prisoners had been cut on 1 June by order of the commissary-general of prisoners in retaliation for reports of conditions in the Confederate prisoner of war camp in Andersonville, Georgia. Additionally, on 10 August Hoffman prohibited the shipping of supplies, other than clothing, from relatives and friends to the prisoners. Confederates that had enlisted in the Union army, however, were no longer considered prisoners, but "enlisted men" and received full rations. According to one prisoner, "Never since the Son of Man was tempted by the Devil, was dishonor more cunningly devised or temptingly displayed." 47/

Prisoner opinions aside, it is doubtful that the motivation for the hardships put upon them was to encourage enlistments. Both Secretary of War Stanton and General Grant were opposed to the recruitment of prisoners, but deferred to the president. As it proved, the prisoners recruited in September and October of 1864 were allowed to sit where they were until the latter part of February 1865, before being organized. This proved to be an administrative nightmare to Colonel Johnson, who wrote to the commissary-general of prisoners in December that:

> . . . The 1,797 enlisted men recruited from the prisoners here still occupy a large portion of the prison, separated from the prisoners by a high board fence, and sixteen barracks are contained in this division and occupied by these recruits. This you will perceive is a serious reduction from the capacity of the prison, and the object of keeping these men here cannot be fathomed. Their condition is deplorable, as they are poorly clad and clothing cannot be issued to them from the prisoners' stock, as they are no longer prisoners. Clothing cannot be issued to them from the quartermaster's department, as they are not organized . . . 48/

Additionally, over 1,000 prisoners at Rock Island had answered the Union call to arms in the spring of 1864, when even those prisoners most highly critical of the camp agree that rations were abundant. While some prisoners may have been "starved" into submission by the cut in provisions, the major motivation for prisoners becoming "Galvanized Yankees," as they were later known, was probably a realization that the South could no longer win the war, and that the only way to effect an early release from confinement, given the breakdown of the exchange program, was to enlist. Ironically, the exchange of prisoners with the South was reinstituted about the same time as the "Galvanized Yankees" were organized and shipped west.

Beginning as early as January 1864, rumors circulated about the conditions existing within the prison camp on Rock Island; in the beginning concentrating on the high mortality rate from disease, and calling for improvements in the prison's medical facilities and staff. By June, however, the papers had begun to publish stories of "deliberate murder" of prisoners by parapet guards, but still supported the officers in charge of the camp, attributing the shooting in question to an "indiscreet act of a raw soldier who had not sufficient judgement to perform his duty properly." 49/

Amicable relations between the prison staff and the Rock Island Argus were severed, however, in November 1864, when the newspaper published a report of conditions on the island which contended that:

> . . . the prisoners are kept on too short fare, in fact they are starved down to barely a living point; that they are allowed no vegetables, and only a small 8 ounce loaf of bread and a piece of salt meat about as big as your two fingers for the whole 24 hours. Under this scanty and unsuitable fare they are pining away, becoming diseased, and fast filling the hospitals and grave yards. Under this treatment, that dreadful scourge, the scurvey, has made its appearance among them, and they now have a place set apart for the scurvey patients. . .

The *Argus* lamented that:

> . . . It is a shame that, in this enlightened age of the world, white men, our own countrymen, should be confined in a pen, fed on such scanty and improper food, and reduced down almost to starvation point, until disease and death ensue. . . If done by order of the administration it is a shame and a disgrace to the party in power. If done by the officers in charge of the prison it is a shame and a disgrace to them. There is no excuse for this deliberate torture of human beings, and the hand that does it or the heart that prompts it is hardened against the common instincts of humanity. . . 50/

Shortly thereafter, the *Argus* published a response to the article penned by a furious Colonel Johnson. "Up to the present time I have passed unnoticed the numerous erroneous articles that have appeared in the papers in this vicinity in relation to the occurences at this Post," he wrote, "but in this case I will deviate from an established rule, and give your article of the 21st inst. the notice it seems to merit." Johnson then denied the allegations of mistreatment, and maintained that the treatment of prisoners at Rock Island and all issues to them were "made strictly in accordance with orders from the War Department." 51/

Johnson also roundly condemned the *Argus* for allegedly ignoring the suffering of Union prisoners in Southern prisons and of sympathizing with the rebel cause. Finally, with more righteous outrage than tact, Johnson stated what his actions in regard to the treatment of Southern prisoners would be if the "discretionary power" rested with him.

> . . . In the first place, instead of placing them in fine comfortable barracks, with three large stoves in each, and as much coal as they can burn, both day and night, I would place them in a pen with no shelter but

Colonel Adolphus J. Johnson
Commanding Officer
Rock Island Barracks

the heavens, as our poor men were at Andersonville; instead of giving them the same quality and nearly the same quantity of provisions that the troops on duty receive, I would give them as near as possible the same quantity and quality of provisions that the fiendish rebels give our men; and instead of a constant issue of clothing to them I would let them wear their rags, as our poor men in the hands of rebel authorities are obliged to do. . . 52/

Thusly are ogres created; for in all the criticism of the camp leveled by ex-inmates at the turn of the century, the only substantial bit of evidence backing allegations that guards were ordered to indiscriminately shoot at prisoners and that Johnson, himself, was "as inhuman a brute as ever disgraced a uniform," was a paragraph penned in anger by a harassed and frustrated officer. 53/

Colonel Johnson's war record shows him to be less the ogre his critics would make him out to be. Born in 1816, he was a merchant in Newark, New Jersey, at the outbreak of the Civil War. He reacted to the fall of Fort Sumpter by marching off to Trenton and enlisting in the First Regiment New Jersey Militia, of which he was commissioned colonel and commander. When the First was mustered out at the end of three months service in Washington, Johnson was commissioned as the Colonel commanding the Eighth New Jersey in September 1861. After serving in the defense of Washington throughout the winter of 1861-62, the Eighth New Jersey participated in General George McClellan's Penninsular Campaign in Virginia. There, Johnson fought in the siege of Yorktown during April and early May, but was severely wounded during the Battle of Williamsburg on 5 May 1862 when he was haplessly shot in the back with a minie ball. After convalescing in New Jersey for five months, he rejoined his regiment with his wound still open, in time to participate in the Battle of Fredericksburg. By March 1863 his wound had closed, but it left him generally weak and unable to "endure even the necessary duties of camp service." Not wishing to remain in the army "unless prepared for all duties," Johnson resigned on 12 March 1863. 54/

Johnson's physical condition began to improve, however, and he was commissioned as a major in the Veteran Reserve Corps in July 1863, and as a colonel on 28 September. After serving for two months at Camp Chase, Ohio, another Union prison camp, Johnson was sent to Rock Island to serve under Colonel Richard H. Rush, the organizer of the Corps, who served as the camp's commanding officer until Johnson assumed command on 5 December 1863. Rush described Johnson as "a very superior officer" who would be "fully able to carry on this establishment." 55/

It is hardly in keeping with his image as an "inhuman brute," that Johnson telegrammed the following to Hoffman in May 1865: "2/3rds of Prisoners released under order of 9th inst[ant] are destitute - can hard bread be furnished them to their homes?" 56/

After the war ended, rumors about the Rock Island Barracks continued to spread, fueled by an occasional newspaper article. In July 1867, the Argus asserted that the "Two thousand dead confederates, now mouldering to dust, on the Island, attest that greater numbers died here than in Andersonville or any other southern prison, in proportion to the number confined and the time occupied." 57/

Starting around the turn of the century and continuing into the 1920s, Confederate Veteran magazine published a series of articles written by former prisoners at Rock Island, which to a great extent condemned the prison for wantonly shooting prisoners, starving them in an attempt to gain recruits to the Union army, and for employing "every devilish device that could be conjured up in the brain of a savage" to make prisoners suffer. Margaret Mitchell, in writing her monumental, though somewhat historically inaccurate, epic, Gone With the Wind, drew on these accounts to mollify Southern consciences on their own treatment of prisoners of war. Mitchell wrote:

> . . . inflamed by reports from Andersonville, the north resorted to harsher treatment of Confederate prisoners and at no place were conditions worse than at Rock Island. Food was scanty, one blanket for three men, and the ravages of smallpox, pneumonia and typhoid gave the place the name of a pesthouse. Three-fourths of all the men sent there never came out alive.

Thus firmly established, the myth of the "Andersonville of the North" continued to flourish as late as 1969, when the Davenport Times Democrat published a fictionalized account of the prison drawing predominately from the Confederate Veteran articles. 58/

Conditions within the camp were harsh. A rebel soldier violating the camp's regulations or attempting to escape was subject to a number of punitive measures including being marched in place for several hours at a stretch, being strapped by the thumbs or wrists to the fence and forced to stand on tip-toe for several hours, being ball and chained, or being treated to a ride on "Morgan's mule." This last device, named after the Confederate general who raided across the Ohio River, was a one-inch board set on its edge at a height of about eight feet above the ground. Prisoners were forced to straddle this device for several hours, resulting in severe discomfort. (See illustrations on pages 14 and 30). 59/

Yet, Union guards were subjected to the same punishments as the prisoners. Flogging had been banned in 1861, but other forms of corporal punishment were in widespread use during the Civil War. On 14 April 1865, Private George W. Shultz of the camp's guard force was fined $16 and condemned to be "tied up to a tree by the hands for two hours" as punishment for assault and drunkenness. Additionally, a surviving photograph of the Union guardhouse at Vicksburg show Union troops riding a device strikingly similar to "Morgan's Mule." 60/

At times, the guard force seemed to be more "mistreated" than the prisoners. In January 1865 the following order was posted:

> The prevalent habit of committing nuisances about the island by the enlisted men of this and other commands has rendered it necessary that stringent measures be taken to correct it. Accordingly tomorrow the Guard on the Parapet will be instructed to fire upon any man seen committing any nuisance outside of the privies. Company Commanders will cause this order to be read to their respective companies at least once a day, today and for the next seven successive days.

It is not recorded that anyone was dispatched in this less than honorable fashion, however. 61/

In addition to punitive measures for misbehavior, the camp imposed hardship on the prisoners for simply being "rebels." The commissary-general of prisoners required each camp to establish a "prison fund" to pay for "all such articles as may be necessary for the health and comfort of the prisoners and which would otherwise have to be purchased by the Government." This fund was used for "table furniture and cooking utensils, articles for policing purposes, bedticks and straw, the means of improving or enlarging the barrack accomodations," and additional pay for prisoner-clerks who kept the camp post office and accounts of the prisoners' money. Unfortunately, this fund was raised by returning to the commissary the difference in rations between that allowed for Union troops and that allowed for prisoners. Needed construction, such as the building of the prison hospital, came at the cost of reduced rations. The further reduction in rations ordered in retaliation for conditions at Andersonville created further hardships, and assertions that prisoners would capture and eat unwary dogs and rats abounded. The fiscally conservative Colonel Hoffman closely watched each expenditure from the fund. As a consequence, while over $87,000 was spent at Rock Island for the "benefit of the prisoners," $174,000 was returned to the subsistence department at the end of the war. In all, Hoffman returned almost $1,900,000 which could have been spent to relieve the sufferings of Confederate prisoners in the North. 62/

Roll call near western gate. Note "Morgan's Mule" in foreground and ditch to discourage tunneling.

Contrary to the opinions of its critics, the Rock Island Barracks was one of the better prisoner of war camps in the country. Its mortality rate over its twenty-month existence (expressed in the number of deaths per thousand prisoners per year) was 193.2 -- below that for the average Union prison camp, which was 230.4, and far below that for Andersonville, which was 732.6. Even more significantly, during the twelve month period from April 1864 to March 1865, after the smallpox plague was more or less under control and before the prisoner population dropped to below 5,000, the camp experienced a death rate of 133.3; significantly lower than the death rate from disease experienced by Confederate troops in the field, which was 167.3. While shootings of prisoners did exist, J. W. Minnich, one of the harshest of the Confederate Veteran critics of the camp recounts only 12 shootings, 9 of which resulted in fatalities, and three of those occured during escape attempts. Moreover, the other chief complaint, the scarcity of food after June 1864, was the work of the secretary of war, and beyond the control of the camp's administration. While malnutrition was no doubt a major problem, only 12 deaths were attributed to scurvy, and the drop in the death rate during this period of privation belies contentions of widespread starvation. 63/

Several factors went into the propagation of the "Andersonville of the North" myth. One involved the quality and nature of the guard force which was assigned to secure the camp.

The original guard force was the Fourth Regiment of the Invalid Corps. The corps had been created on 28 April 1863 and was composed of men that had been wounded or were ill, and were judged to be no longer capable of duty in line regiments. Unfortunately, the initials "I.C." they wore on their light blue uniforms also stood for "Inspected, Condemned" which the Quartermaster Corps would stamp on unserviceable equipment. After a year of unmerciful kidding from other soldiers and the general public, the name of the corps was changed to the Veteran Reserve Corps. Yet, if this group received little respect from outside the camp, within it they were appreciated. Even Minnich states that "as a rule they were decent in their treatment of us. I have no complaint to lay against them. They were veterans. . ." 64/

But problems began when elements of the Veteran Reserve Corps were replaced by the 37th Iowa (Gray Beards). The unit had been formed in December 1862 to free other troops for combat, and was composed of men over the age of 45. Indeed, one recruit, Curtis King of Muscatine, was eighty. By their arrival in Rock Island, however, their initial enthusiasm had faded, and a good many were anxious to be mustered out. The conditions they found at the barracks, recounted on page 3, had a devastating toll on their morale and health, and contributed to their becoming a "regiment of decrepit old men." By the time the regiment was ordered to Memphis in June 1864, their discipline had deteriorated to such an extent that the regiment's executive officer was under arrest. 65/

The regiment's morale problems were, in great part, due to the nature of its commanding officer. Colonel George Washington Kincaid, a pioneer farmer from Muscatine County, Iowa, and a member of the state's first constitutional convention, was a "forceful man of extremes" and an adamant teetotaler. One of his men described him as being:

> . . . uninviting in personal appearance and in address. He was strict in his discipline, to which may be attributed his great unpopularity with his regiment. I am unwilling to record the many stories of his misrule. . . In the judgement of his regiment, he served with little honor to himself or his state." 66/

Upon his arrival at Rock Island, Colonel Kincaid immediately locked horns with Colonel Johnson over not being quartered on the island, and complained to the secretary of war. Both Stanton and Henry W. Halleck, the army's general in chief, demanded explanations from the harrassed Johnson. His reply illuminates Kincaid's character.

> . . . Could not quarter the 37th Iowa Regt on the Island, for every Barrack was filled. . . Did quarter them in good buildings at Rock Island City. [Captain Charles A.] Reynolds then Telegraphed to Washington that they were so quartered, and at heavy expense to the Government and suggested that as Camp Roberts near Davenport, was vacant that the Regt be sent there. Gen Halleck replied "Send the 37th Iowa Regt to Camp Roberts." Col Kincaid of 37th refused to move his command there. Capt Reynolds Telegraphed his refusal to the Department. No orders have since been received about them.

Johnson had the last laugh, however, when the 37th was moved into quarters on the island; in the compound with the prisoners. Elements of the regiment remained there until 10 May 1864. 67/

The 37th Iowa was replaced by a succession of volunteer regiments of troops that had enlisted for 100 days, including the 133rd Illinois, the 48th Iowa, and the 197th Pennsylvania. The "100 days men" were of questionable military value at best, and quickly got the reputation of being too quick to shoot at prisoners, and of shooting into the barracks at night. According to Minnich, "Their firing into the barracks during the night became a matter of such common occurrence that men in the outer rows next to the dead line feared to sleep on the upper and middle bunks, and slept on the floor in many instances." However, apparently only one man was wounded from this series of shootings and that was attributed to an accidental discharge of a weapon. 68/

The firing the prisoners heard at night may have been from guards emptying their weapons, which were smooth bore muskets that could not be unloaded and had to be fired to clear them. This problem posed a perennial problem for Colonel Johnson who had forbidden the discharge of any weapons except with the guard being relieved in the mornings. The "hundred days men" were less disciplined than previous guards, though, and on 11 June 1864, the Davenport Democrat reported that men engaged in quarrying rock on the riverbank just above east Davenport:

> . . . have been annoyed and seriously endangered by the discharge of fire arms by the guards to the rebel barracks on Rock Island, who have been in the habit of firing across the river . . . The shooting was done by some of the hundred days men, who like children with new toys are unduly anxious to test the merit of their rifles.

The situation was so serious, that Major Charles P. Kingsbury, the arsenal commander, wrote to Colonel Johnson and requested that he "give such orders as will prevent a recurrence of such reckless conduct, and enable the workmen to resume their labors." 69/

What appeared to be maleficence, however, could have been merely bad marksmanship. Guards coming off duty were marched to the east end of the island, and there fired their weapons at a target to clear them. But they had a persistent habit of missing the target, and sending rounds in any direction. A frustrated Johnson would eventually write the following:

> The carelessness of the Guard in discharging their pieces at the target has been the source of many complaints to these Headquarters, which have shown that if life has not been lost it was not for the want of opportunity.

Johnson then ordered the officer of the guard to march the guard being relieved to the target ground, and to personally insure that each musket was aimed at the target. 70/

Contemporary drawing of post (garrison) hospital.

Yet, if the prisoners disliked the "100 days men," the situation, from their point of view anyway, would become worse. On 24 September 1864, Lafayette Rogan noted in his diary that a regiment of "contrabands" had arrived for garrison duty, and on 26 September, he reported that "8,000 Southern men to day are guarded by their slaves who have been armed by the Tyrant." 71/

The arrival of the 108th Regiment, US Colored Infantry, which had been recruited from the slave population of northern and west-central Kentucky in June and July of 1864, infuriated the Confederate prisoners, who considered the move as an insult directed towards them. In the prisoners' view, the black guards were sub-human. Minnich's description of one of them is illustrative.

> . . . [He was] a squat-built negro as black as any ever painted by nature's brush, low forehead, deep-set eyes, and the elongated jaw of the gorilla, a face denoting at once the low grade of mentality characteristic of the lowest type of the negro--a mere brute. 72/

Given the antipathy of the guards held by the prisoners, and the strong possibility of resentment of the prisoners by the guards, it is understandable that flare-ups would occur. Plans were made to throw rocks at the black sentries on the wall, though Minnich contends that "wiser councils prevailed, and the matter was dropped." But it is beyond doubt that prisoners verbally harassed the guards and refused to obey orders given by them. The prisoners also contended that on several occasions, black guards would accept bribes from prisoners to allow escapees to safely scale the prison wall, then shoot the prisoners. Guards would also fire at stiff-necked prisoners who refused to obey their orders. Finally, it became almost a standard charge by ex--prisoners that the guards were shooting on the orders of Colonel Johnson, himself, though all evidence points to the contrary. 73/

The 108th was also subjected to discrimination by their comrades in arms. The arrival of the 108th was greeted by the establishment of a Jim Crow ward in the post (garrison) hospital, and its commander, Lieutenant Colonel John Bishop complained that his men were used too often for fatigue details, and that no efforts were being made to improve their quarters area. Even in death, the 108th suffered less than equal treatment. In the national cemetery, the 50 graves of those that died while serving at the prison are in a separate section from the other guard regiments. Ironically, the 16 "Galvanized Yankees" that died before they were shipped west are buried with the guards of the 108th. 74/

In addition, the 108th came into conflict with inhabitants of the City of Davenport, who were less than generous in their descriptions of the soldiers. In January 1865 the Davenport Democrat published the following:

> A DARK TRANSACTION--Two darkies having trespassed on the laws by stealing and riotous conduct in this city, thereby getting themselves locked up in jail, a squad of their dark brethren, some forty strong, who stand guard for a living, on the Island, managed to escape from their quarters last evening and came to Davenport with arms in their hands and wool erect, for the purpose of rescuing their brethren, or to perish in the attempt. . . These "black boys in blue" are getting to think less of "white trash" than ever. It seems as though there was a screw loose on the Island, else so many would not have been allowed to come over here at once to startle the usual peaceful citizens of Davenport into such fearful commotion. . .

As a consequence of this friction, Bishop prohibited his men from visiting Davenport until the middle of May. 75/

The antipathy between the civilian population and the black regiment was not so evident on the Illinois shore of the river, because when the regiment began to embark for Vicksburg in the latter part of May 1865, the Argus noted that the "colored soldiers, as a general thing, have conducted themselves with great propriety, since they were stationed here." 76/

Another factor in the propagation of the "Andersonville of the North" myth was the frequency of inaccurate reportage in the area newspapers, exacerbated by the rivalry between towns and between the newspapers themselves. In April 1864 the Davenport Democrat published an article entitled "UGH!" which stated that all the "offal and garbage" produced by the 7,000 prisoners on the island was being drained directly into Sylvan Slough, which swept it to the City of Rock Island, "impregnating the waters which her citizens use and breeding disease and contagion generally." The Democrat warned that the "traveling public should avoid such a place and come to Davenport where they can find first class accomodations and pure water." And in March 1865 the Democrat published the absurd charge that surgeons at the prison barracks were selling the bodies of deceased rebel prisoners to area physicians for the purpose of disection. 77/

The Argus was not above reproach, either. In March 1864 it picked up a rumor at the camp and published the following account:

> . . . We learn that, last night, one of the prisoners of war at Rock Island Barracks gave birth to a fine healthy boy, quite to the astonishment of her comrades who had not until then, suspected her sex. The affair created considerable excitement at the Barracks. We presume that Col. Johnson will see that the mother and child receive such care as humanity will dictate, under the circumstances.

Lafayette Rogan clarified the mystery when he noted in his diary, "The story of the birth in prison has been magnified and transmorgified from a puppy to a baby--The truth however, did not come out until the story appeared in the daily Argus of Rock Island." 78/

Politics also played a role in newspaper coverage of the prison. The Argus and the Democrat backed the Democratic candidacy of George B. McClellan in the presidential election of 1864, and tended to overplay conditions at the camp to embarrass the Lincoln administration. Conversely, the pro-Republican Rock Island Union was generally uncritical of the camp and the administration. 79/

Another reason for the "Andersonville of the North" myth lay within the psyches of the Southerners themselves.

Henry Wirz, the commandant of the infamous prison camp in Georgia, had been faced with many of the problems that had plagued the Rock Island camp. But, unlike Johnson, Wirz was also plagued with severe overcrowding. The 16 1/2 acre enclosure was first established in February 1864, and was designed to hold 10,000 prisoners. Yet by May over 15,000 were crowded into the stockade, which was still devoid of barracks or huts, and prisoners were arriving at the rate of 400 per day. By midsummer the enclosure had been expanded an additional ten acres, but the prison population was now over 30,000. The severe overcrowding, exacerbated by the ensuing contagion and the South's inability to provide adequate shelter or anything above a meager diet, caused the Union prisoners incarcerated at Andersonville to die off at a rate of 100 per day. 80/

Popular outrage at the deaths at Andersonville, which by the end of the war numbered 13,000, demanded that the camp's unfortunate commandant be tried and hanged for his crimes. Southern outrage at the hanging of Wirz, together with their own feelings of guilt over the realities of Andersonville, created a need in the Southern psyche to demonstrate that the South was not alone in the mistreatment of prisoners of war, that Wirz was really used as a scapegoat to soothe Northern consciences, and that in reality, the Northern camps were worse than Andersonville

itself. By emphasizing the brutalities of northern prisons, Southern guilt over the existence of Andersonville could be assuaged. 81/

There is some validity to the Southern argument, however. All Civil War prison camps were "Andersonvilles," to some extent or another, though none approached the hellishness of the original. In the words of noted Civil War historian Bruce Catton:

> Each government, the one at Washington and the one at Richmond, was straining itself and its country's economy to conduct the war. Each government had many things to think of--raising and supporting armies, providing food and munitions and equipment, maintaining its finances and its industries and its transportation system, trying in short to handle an all-out war for which there had been no preparation of any consequence. In all of this, on each side, the conduct of the prison camps usually came last. Whatever time, money, energy, and administrative competence were left over, after the business of fighting the war was taken care of, could be applied to the care of prisoners. As the record proves, this was not nearly enough.
>
> Under any circumstances, indeed, prison camps in that generation were certain to be bad. Even in his own army, when he was far removed from the battlefield and situated where he could get the best care his government could give him, the Civil War soldier existed under conditions that were just barely endurable. His food was bad, his housing was usually atrocious, his medical care was cruelly imperfect; disease and malnutrition killed far more soldiers (leaving those who died in prison entirely out of consideration) than ever died in combat. Just to be in the army at all was a serious danger to life and limb in the 1860's. To be a prisoner of war inevitably intensified that danger, not because anyone planned it that way but simply because it was bound to happen so. 82/

The answer to the question, "Was the Rock Island Prison Barracks the Andersonville of the North?," therefore, is an unequivical yes-and-no. Among a bad lot, the camp, despite its shortcomings, was one of the best. But, while not approaching the degree of death and privation of its Southern counterpart, the camp induced suffering to a degree that makes modern society flinch, despite our memories of more recent camps that were infinitely worse.

The Rock Island Barracks is gone today. With Lee's surrender at Appomattox, the prison camps of the North began to empty as prisoners signed the oath of allegiance and were released. The last two prisoners were dismissed from the prison hospital in July 1865, and Colonel Johnson turned over the camp's buildings to the arsenal, which used them for storage until they were demolished to make way for the arsenal's expansion. The last building, the central administration building of the post (garrison) hospital, disappeared in 1909. 83/

Commissary-General of Prisoners Hoffman was breveted to brigadier general, then to major general for "faithful, meritorious, and distinguished services" during the war. He retired from the army in 1870, then moved to the City of Rock Island, where he died in 1884. He is buried in that city's historic Chippiannock Cemetery. 84/

Colonel Johnson was not as fortunate. After attempting to remain in the army, he was finally mustered out in July 1866 and returned to Newark. He died there in 1893, his brain destroyed by general paresis. In 1904, one of Johnson's ex-charges described him as the "Devil's Archangel." He wrote, "Rock Island has long since passed away as a prison, and it is fervently hoped that the Devil has, also long since, claimed his own." Perhaps, in a way, he had. 85/

The only permanent reminders of the existence of the Rock Island Barracks are the cemeteries that mark the final resting place of the 1,964 Confederate soldiers and the 125 Union guards that died here. Yet the memory of the camp lingers on. Each Memorial Day, the Union guards are honored with the other United States veterans that are buried in the Rock Island National Cemetery. But the veterans of the Confederate States of America are honored as well. A Confederate battle flag is placed on each grave in the Confederate Cemetery, and "Taps" is played once more to honor the dead.

APPENDIX

Camp Statistics

MONTH/YEAR	NUMBER PRISONERS	NUMBER GUARDS	PRISONER DEATHS	GUARD DEATHS
Nov/1863	0	823	0	0
Dec/1863	5,592	1,342	98	3
Jan/1864	7,912	1,359	231	4
Feb/1864	7,596	1,427	350	10
Mar/1864	7,225	1,761	288	14
Apr/1864	6,933	1,775	141	3
May/1864	7,177	1,760	78	6
Jun/1864	8,594	1,964	100	4
Jul/1864	8,572	1,489	73	6
Aug/1864	8,385	1,987	114	6
Sep/1864	8,260	2,388	71	1
Oct/1864	8,167	1,841	51	13
Nov/1864	6,381	1,662	41	13
Dec/1864	6,724	1,594	100	9
Jan/1865	6,625	1,534	109	10
Feb/1865	6,271	1,539	57	5
Mar/1865	5,079	1,522	33	8
Apr/1865	2,762	1,513	20	7
May/1865	2,654	871	7	1
Jun/1865	1,102	801	2	2
Jul/1865	2	61	0	0
Aug/1865	0	54	0	0

```
TOTAL PRISONERS HELD   12,192
TRANSFERRED               730
EXCHANGED               3,876
DIED                    1,964
ESCAPED                    41
RELEASED                5,581
```

NOTES

1/LTC George G. Lewis and CPT John Mewha, History of Prisoner of War Utilization by the United States Army: 1776-1945 (Department of the Army Pamphlet No. 20-213), pp. 29-30; Frank L. Byrne, "Prison Pens of Suffering," in William C. Davis, ed., The Image of War:1861-1865 Volume IV Fighting for Time (Garden City, NY: Doubleday & Company, Inc., 1983), p. 401.

2/T. R. Walker, "Rock Island Prison Barracks" in William B. Hesseltine, Civil War Prisons (Kent, Ohio: Kent State University Press, 1962), p. 48.

3/Rock Island Argus, 31 July 1863.

4/Walker, pp. 48-49.

5/Ibid., p. 49; Rock Island Argus, 18 November 1863; Davenport Democrat, 20 January 1864; BG Fred C. Ainsworth and Joseph W. Kirkley, comp., The War of the Rebellion: A Compilation of the Official Records of the Union and Confederate Armies (Washington: Government Printing Office, 1899), Series II, hereinafter cited as OR, Vol. VII, p. 23; Rock Island Argus, 23 May 1864; Walker, p. 51.

6/Mrs. Kate E. Perry-Mosher, "History of Rock Island, ILL., 1863," Confederate Veteran, January 1906, p. 28.

7/Telegram, Colonel Richard H. Rush to Colonel William Hoffman, dated 4 December 1863, found in National Archives, Record Group 393 (hereinafter referred to as NARG 393), Volume 4, Entries 1080 and 1082; Davenport Democrat, 30 December 1863; Rock Island Argus, 4 January 1864; Ibid., 5 January 1864.

8/Walker, p. 49; Ibid., p. 50; Bryan England, "Arsenal prison called the Andersonville of the North," Rock Island Arsenal Target, 8 March 1985, p. 7.

9/Ibid.; OR, Vol. VII, pp. 13. The guards were reinterred in the national cemetery after the war.

10/George W. Cullum, Biographical Register of the Officers and Graduates of the U. S. Military Academy at West Point, N. Y. From its Establishment, in 1802, to 1890 Volume I (Cambridge: The Riverside Press, 1891), p. 433; "An Eventful Life," Davenport Democrat, 13 August 1884, p. 1; OR, Vol. IV, p. 30.

11/OR, Vol. VII, pp. 12-13; Ibid., Vol. VII, p. 13; Ibid., p. 15.

12/Ibid., p. 16.

13/Ibid., pp. 24-25.

14/Ibid., p. 26; Ibid., p. 27.

15/Ibid., p. 29.

16/Ibid., p. 59.

17/Ibid., p. 65; Ibid.

18/Ibid.; Monthly return, June 1864, found in *Monthly Returns from U.S., Military Posts: Rock Island Barracks, November, 1863--August, 1865* (National Archives Microfilm Publications, Washington, D.C.) Reel 1037, hereinafter referred to as Monthly or Tri-monthly returns.

19Lafayette Rogan, *Diary of Lafayette Rogan*, typescript in Historical Office, Army Armament, Munitions, and Chemical Command (AMCCOM), p. 34; OR, Vol. VII, pp. 196-7.

20/OR, Vol. VII, p. 507.

21/Ibid., p. 506; Ibid., p. 507.

22/Ibid., Vol. VIII, pp. 993-7.

23/Walker, p. 54; Quoted in Carl McIntire, "'Recollections of Rock Island Prison' tells of hardships experienced by Confederates," Jackson, MS, *Clarion-Ledger--Jackson Daily News*, 9 December 1984, p. 6H.

24/OR, Vol. VII, pp. 180-1; Lewis and Mewha, p. 39.

25/Clifford Stephens, *Rock Island Prison Barracks: 1863--1865* (Rock Island Arsenal Pamphlet No. 870-3: March 20, 1967) p. 11.

26/Dr. Thomas F. Berry, "Prison Experiences on Rock Island," *Confederate Veteran*, February 1912, pp. 65 and 67-69.

27/Rock Island Barracks, IL, *General Register of Prisoners: 1864-1865* (National Archives Microfilm Publications, Washington, D.C.), Microcopy 598, Reel 131.

28/B. M. Hord, "Forty Hours in a Dungeon at Rock Island," *Confederate Veteran*, August 1904, pp. 386-7.

29/Rock Island Barracks, IL, *Guard Reports*, National Archives Record Group (NARG) 393, Volume 4, Entry 1089; Berry, pp. 65-66.

30/*OR*, Vol. VII, p. 415. The prisoner reported as having drowned was actually one of the seven recaptured. The remaining three were captured at Mt. Pleasant, Iowa, by a "vigilance committee." Letter, Johnson to Hoffman, 12 July 1864, NARG 393, Volume 4, Entry 1078, p. 102.

31/Letter, Johnson to Hoffman, 25 January 1865, NARG 393, Volume 4, Entry 1078, p. 153.

32/Rock Island *Daily Union*, 13 March 1916, p. 31.

33/Rock Island *Union*, 13 January 1864, quoted in Rock Island *Argus*, 18 January 1864. "Secesh" was a derogatory abbreviation of "Secessionist."

34/Perry-Mosher, p. 28.

35/Rogan, p. 9.

36/Perry-Mosher, p. 29.

37/Ibid. See also, Letter, Johnson to Hoffman, 15 September 1864, NARG 393, Volume 4, Entry 1078, p. 118.

38/*OR*, Vol. VIII, pp. 523-5; Ibid., p. 896.

39/Rock Island *Daily Union*, 3 October 1915.

40/*OR*, Vol. VII, p. 537; Telegram, John T. Brooks to Johnson, 13 October 1864, NARG 393, Volume 4, Entry 1080 & 1082; Rock Island Barracks, IL, Special Orders Number 7, dated 13 January 1865, in NARG 393, Volume 4, Entries 1083-1085.

41/Lewis and Mewha, pp. 31-36.

42/Rock Island *Argus*, 19 January 1864; Ibid., 20 January 1864.

43/Rock Island *Argus*, 1 February 1864; Rogan, p. 7; Rock Island *Argus*, 1 August 1864.

44/Lewis and Mewha, p. 34.

45/Rogan, p. 50; OR, Vol. VII, p. 1245.

46/Ibid.

47/OR, Vol. VIII, p. 38; Rock Island Argus, 22 August 1864; Hord, p. 385.

48/Lewis and Mewha, p. 35; Tri-monthly returns, 20 February 1864 and 28 February 1865; OR, Vol. VII, p. 1245. Lincoln wrote to Grant and apologized for the recruitment, terming it a "blunder." OR, Series III, Volume IV, p. 740.

49/Rock Island Argus, 2 January 1864; Ibid., 14 June 1864.

50/Rock Island Argus, 21 November 1864; Ibid.

51/Rock Island Argus, 26 November 1864.

52/Ibid.

53/Hord, p. 385.

54/NARG 15, Civil War Pension File, Adolphus J. Johnson, WC 385 967; NARG 94, Compiled Service Record (Union), A. J. Johnson, 4th VRC; NARG 94, Compiled Service Record (Union), Adolphus J. Johnson, 8th New Jersey Infantry; William S. Stryker, Record of the Officers and Men of New Jersey in the Civil War, 1861-1865 Volume I (Trenton, NJ: John L. Murphy, Steam Book and Job Printer, 1876), pp. 15 and 366.

55/Ibid.; Letter, Rush to Colonel James B. Fry, dated 26 November 1863, NARG 393, Volume 4, Entry 1078, p. 13. Rush, the son of the American envoy and minister to the Court of St. James, was an 1846 graduate of West Point; graduating behind Cadets George B. McClellan (number 2) and Thomas J. Jackson (number 17), but ahead of Cadet George E. Pickett, who graduated at the bottom of the list. Rush resigned from the army on 1 July 1864. Cullum, Volume II, p. 276.

56/Telegram, Johnson to Hoffman, 19 May 1865, NARG 393, Volume 4, Entries 1080 and 1082.

57/Rock Island Argus, 24 July 1867.

58/Hord, p. 385; Quoted in George W. Wickstrom, The Town Crier (Rock Island, IL: The J. W. Potter Company, 1948), p. 167. The death rate Mitchell cites came from "Marking Graves of Confederate Prisoners," Confederate Veteran, March 1904, p. 102.

Mitchell apparently missed B. M. Hord's rebuttal of the figures which appeared in "Marking Graves of Confederate Prisoners," Confederate Veteran, May 1904, p. 225; Davenport Times Democrat, 16 February 1969, p. 1D.

59/E. Polk Johnson, "Some Prison Experiences," Confederate Veteran, January 1919, p. 5; England, op. cit., p. 7.

60/Fred Albert Shannon, The Organization and Administration of the Union Army 1861-1865 (2 Volumes, Cleveland: The Arthur H. Clark Company, 1928), Volume I, pp. 175 and 226. Rock Island Barracks, IL, General Order Number 16, dated 14 April 1865, NARG 393, Volume 4, Entries 1083-1085; England, p. 7.

61/Regimental Orders Number 5, dated 22 January 1865, Order Book, 108 US Colored Infantry, NARG 94: Records of the Adjutant General's Office.

62/Circular, Office Commissary-General of Prisoners, dated 7 July 1862, NARG 249, Office of the Commissary General of Prisoners; Rogan, p. 64; Hord, p. 386; Consolidated Statement of Prison and Parole Camp Funds during the Secession Rebellion, NARG 249, Office of the Commissary General of Prisoners.

63/Charles Smart, The Medical and Surgical History of the War of the Rebellion, Part III, Volume I (Washington: Government Printing Office, 1888), p. 48 and 61; J. W. Minnich, Inside of Rock Island Prison from December, 1863 to June, 1865 (Nashville, TN: Publishing House of the M. E. Church, 1908), passim. Rock Island Barracks statistics are derived from "Abstract from monthly returns of the principal U.S. military prisons," found in OR, Series II, Volume VIII, pp. 986-1004; and from Rock Island Barracks, IL, Record of Prisoners of War Who Have Died at Rock Island Barracks, Illinois, (National Archives Microfilm Publications, Washington, D.C.), Microcopy 598, Reel 132.

64/Phillip Katcher, "'They were well thought of...' The Veteran Reserve Corps 1863-1866," Military Images, July-August 1984, pp. 21-22; Minnich, p. 15.

65/George F. Skich, "The Golden Age Regiment: Iowa's Graybeards," Civil War Times Illustrated, May 1981, p. 32; Ibid., pp. 34-35; Monthly return, June 1864. The octogenarian King never made it to Rock Island. Discharged for disability in March 1863, he died in July of that year. Nick Lamberto, "Civil War 'Graybeard's' grave untended," Des Moines (IA) Register, 29 April 1980, p. 1B.

66/Skich, pp. 32 and 44.

67/Telegram, Stanton to Johnson, dated 19 January 1864; Telegram, Halleck to Johnson, dated 20 January 1864; Letter, Johnson to Colonel E. D. Townsend, dated 7 February 1864, all in NARG 393, Volume 4, Entries 1080 and 1082; Letter, Johnson to Kincaid, dated 9 May 1864, NARG 393, Volume 4, Entries 1078, 1079, and 1080.

68/Minnich, p. 34; Rock Island Argus, 1 August 1864.

69/Rock Island Barracks, IL, Post Order Number 77, dated 7 April 1864, NARG 393, Volume 4, Entries 1083-85, p. 54; Davenport Democrat, 11 June 1864; Typescript of letter, Kingsbury to Johnson, 10 June 1864, in Historical Office, AMCCOM.

70/Rock Island Barracks, IL, General Order Number 1, dated 13 January 1865, NARG 393, Volume 4, Entries 1083-85.

71/Rogan, p. 52; Ibid., p. 53.

72/Bruce Wine, "Black Regiment Guarded Prisoners Here," Rock Island Arsenal Target, 2 February 1979, p. 5; Minnich, p. 32.

73/J. W. Minnich, "Comment on Rock Island Prison," Confederate Veteran, August 1908, p. 394.

74/Rock Island Argus, 20 September 1864; Wine, p. 5.

75/Davenport Democrat, 10 January 1865.

76/Undated extract of Rock Island Argus article, Historical Office, AMCCOM.

77/Davenport Democrat, 21 April 1864; Ibid., 28 March 1865.

78/Rock Island Argus, 30 March 1864; Rogan, p. 17.

79/Bryan England, "Sensational newspaper accounts fuel prison myth," Rock Island Arsenal Target, 5 April 1985, p. 7.

80/Bruce Catton, "Prison Camps of the Civil War," American Heritage, August 1959, pp. 7-8.

81/See Minnich, Inside Rock Island Prison, passim.

82/Catton, p. 7.

83/Walker, op. cit., p. 59.

84/Cullum, Volume I, p. 434.

85/Johnson Pension File; Hord, "Marking the Graves," p. 225.

CREDITS

Front Cover -- Contemporary drawing by H. Lambach. National Archives, Center for Cartographic and Architectual Archives, Record Group 77, Miscellaneous Forts File, Ft. Armstrong, IL.

Page 2 -- Historical Office, US Army Armament, Munitions, and Chemical Command, Rock Island, IL.

Page 4 -- Photograph of contemporary lithograph by C. Vogt. John M. Browning Museum, Rock Island Arsenal, Rock Island, IL.

Page 6 -- H. Lambach. National Archives.

Page 8 -- Francis Trevelyan Miller, editor in chief. The Photographic History of the Civil War: Prisons and Hospitals (New York: Castle Books, 1957), p. 53.

Page 14 -- B. F. Tillinghast. Rock Island Arsenal: In Peace and in War (Chicago: The Henry O. Shepard Company, Printers, 1898), p. 32.

Page 20 -- H. Lambach. National Archives.

Page 26 -- Tillinghast, p. 31.

Page 30 -- Illinois State Historical Society.

Page 34 -- H. Lambach. National Archives.

Page 38 -- Miller, p. 131.

Page 40 -- Rock Island Arsenal Photo.